The Memoir of Joey Abo

A Vietnam War-Era Seabee Veteran

By Kimberly Wake

This book is a memoir. It reflects the subject's recollections of his experiences over time. Some names and characteristics have been changed, some events have been compressed, and some dialogue has been recreated.

This memoir is dedicated to my greatest blessings and inspirations - Lisa, my children, and my grandchildren.

Introduction

When my grandchildren were younger, I'd bother them to play a little game. I asked to look at their palms, give them a little squeeze, look off into the distance, and tell them in my best storytelling voice that the lines on their hands say that they have many adventures ahead of them. I could tell by the looks they gave me, usually the eye roll, that they were thinking that Grandpa was just being silly again.

I relish in these moments, however big or small, when my wife and I can wrangle all of the kids and grandkids together in our safe, modest space on the East Coast. Since some of them have moved out of state and have careers and families of their own, this is not always the easiest feat.

All of us love to travel; they most likely got the travel bug from me. When I discovered the world is bigger than a family farm, bigger than surrounding barrios, and that cities bigger than Manila existed, traveling became my passion, and it will be until I can no longer.

So many turns and swirls and potential crashes in my life. I am so grateful for all of them.

My humble beginnings have ingrained modesty.

Love gives me confidence in times of self-doubt.

Family inspires me to go above and beyond. And to set an example.

My faith in God, His Path, and His Light have always been my guides.

As I thumbed through the pages of distant memories for this memoir, all of the emotions came back, too. Some stages were more painful than others to relive, but still, there was something powerful and significant in each. I realize that any variance in decision or event could have changed my whole life's trajectory.

I am where and who I am supposed to be. God willed every single moment.

Chapter One

Farm-to-Table

September 6, 1939 - This is the day I **was blessed with life,** born the fourth child to Leoncia and Venancia Abo in a remote area of the Philippines we know as Barrio Isit, La Paz, Abra[1].

Our living situation was not uncommon in this era and in one of many "backcountry" areas of the Philippines. We were far from being rich money-wise; hard work was not for making a big paycheck. All of the blood, sweat, and sometimes tears that all of us shed as we worked on the farm fed and clothed the family. I suppose you can say our meals were "farm-to-table" in the most genuine sense.

Our old family house can be described as minimalist. Looking back, its simplicity was something of beauty considering all of the love that went into it. My father built it from the ground up.

Sheets of bamboo were supported by strong hardwood posts. Hardwood and bamboo served as smooth, stable flooring for our bare feet. For a roof, my father layered tied bunches of cogon - a waxy, fire-resistant grass native to the Philippines.

We, a family of seven, shared two rooms and one living room. All of us slept on a floor mat woven from palm leaves, each with our own pillow, enshrouded in mosquito netting, as the pesty mini vampires were relentless most of the year.

Our environment blessed us with all of the amenities that were required for us to thrive. Nearby, a large river flowed past our town, and it conveniently served as our toilet, bathtub, and clothing washer.

My father dug a well near our house. This well was about six feet deep, and we needed an average of six full large clay jars of water each day.

Coconuts, which are a staple in the Philippines, were not just used for meat and milk. The durable coconut shells are cleaned and smoothed, and served as cups, bowls, and ladles for soup and water.

My first toothbrush was made from guava twigs, and we used salt as toothpaste. That is, until the end of WWII, when Japanese reparations were distributed to us, and we were introduced to plastic toothbrushes and mint toothpaste, in addition to shelf-stable provisions, such as powdered milk[2].

When darkness fell, we lit coconut oil lamps and kerosene lanterns. Refrigeration was not an option for us at the time, so whatever we gathered, we cooked immediately. Leftovers usually were consumed the next day. One way we kept fish and meat safe to eat for a little longer was to prepare them with plenty of vinegar and salt, which worked as natural preservatives, such as in recipes like "adobo" or "paksiw."[3]

"Cursed is the ground because of you; with hard labor, you shall eat from it all the days of your life"
~ Genesis 3:17, New American Standard Bible

On our farm, we grew rice, corn, eggplant, tomatoes, string beans, cotton, bananas, papaya, guava, sugar cane and gourds as our main crops. The carabaos were used for labor and our hogs were a valuable food source and for selling at the market for profit.

I was four years old when I was considered able-bodied enough to help out on the farm. I started with simply harvesting vegetables. My siblings, Laureana, Aurelia, Emiliano, Joey (Jose), and Prisco, were also each expected to stay on top of their assigned chores around the farm. If anything was neglected, it could have meant failed crops, which would have been devastating to our family's livelihood.

Other special tasks given to my older sisters were weaving fabric and hand-knitting clothing. My mother taught them to loom weave using hardwood weavers. The process of producing fabric took months, depending on how many yards were needed. To begin, we gathered cotton under the cruel heat of the sun for my sisters to tread. Next, we removed the seeds using a cotton gin. We then pounded the cotton with lagundi sticks. The cotton was twisted into yards and yards of yarn with a spindle. A skein rolled the yarn into a loose, oblong-shaped twist. This is the yarn that was woven on hardwood weavers to produce a vibrant, beautiful, and strong fabric that was eventually sewn into garments or household linens.

By the time I was six, I was learning how to plow (*arado*) the field. Plowing started at sunrise and usually ended at sunset. The plow itself was too heavy for me to carry, but the carabaos did the actual pulling as I guided them. My brothers and I helped pasture the carabaos[4]. These giant but gentle creatures were the much-needed muscle on the farm.

When I was not working the fields, my cousins, friends, and I were sharpening our fishing skills, using a variety of methods, such as netting and hook-and-line. This was a lot more fun than plowing! More importantly, it provided another protein source for my family.

This (top) is a typical home found in rural areas of the Philippines. Note the use of bamboo and cogon for the roof. Livestock is usually kept underneath the house.
String beans (bottom left) and eggplant (bottom right).

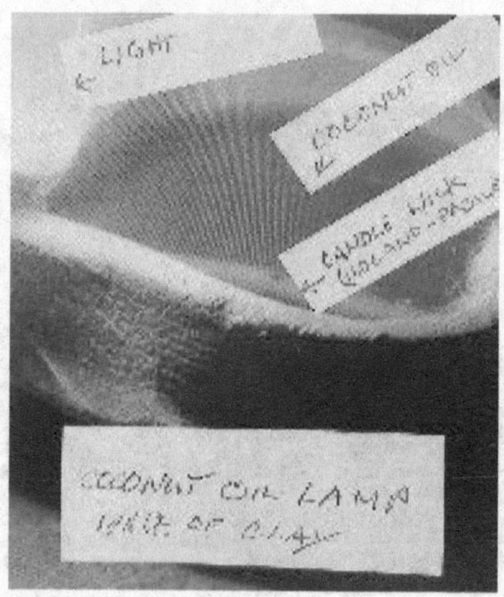

Notes for Context:

[1] Abra is in the midwestern section of the Cordillera Administrative Region in Luzon. It is bordered by the provinces of Ilocos Norte on the northwest, Apayao on the northeast, Kalinga on the mid-east, Mountain Province on the southeast, and Ilocos Sur on the southwest.

[2] In 1942, Japanese forces occupied the Philippines and seized Abra. Abra was liberated by the Philippine Commonwealth forces and local Cordilleran guerrillas during the Battle of Abra in 1945 at the end of WWII. Then, in 1956, Japan and the Philippines signed a Reparations Agreement in accordance with Article 14 (a) 1 of the Peace Treaty. Under this Agreement, Japan provided the Philippines with services and goods valued at the equivalent of $550 million.

[3] Depending on region or family, the basic recipe for adobo is: 1 lb of chicken or pork, 1/4 c of soy sauce, 1/2 c of vinegar, 2 cloves of crushed garlic, 1/2 tsp whole black pepper, 2 bay leaves, 1/2 minced onion and 1 tbsp oil, and salt to taste. In a large pot, sear the meat, then add the rest of the ingredients and stew for at least two hours so that the meat is tender. Serve over rice, of course.

[4] Carabaos are a domesticated species of Asian water buffalo. A variety of sources place their origins from immigrants that vary from Malaysia, Cambodia, China, Spain, and India. Most articles point to Malaysia's introduction that dates all the way back to 300 BC. Carabaos are used mostly for heavy work in agricultural environments, such as for sugar cane and rice, and also, less common, for meat, milk and sport (carabao races).

Chapter Two

A Country of Two Seasons

In the Philippines, there are two truly distinguishable seasons: The rainy season and the dry season. We did not have any nearby grocery stores, so each season dictated the types of crops that were grown and harvested, or were available to purchase or trade at the market.

When it Rains ...

Our rainy season, from June to August, is the season for planting rice and corn. These tasks lasted all day, and we worked every day except for Sundays, our "day of rest" per Catholic tradition[1].

For these crops, we were required to work within the irrigation system, which consisted of deep canals. A common skin condition (*tarim datum*) we got from working in these conditions caused painful welts from our knees down to our feet. We knew of no way to protect ourselves, nor could we refuse to work because of it.

This was also the season in which we were blasted with the most extreme storms. Keep in mind that we didn't have a radio or an alarm system to warn us about oncoming storms. Our only warnings were strong winds, torrential rain, and my parents' gut feelings. My father applied guide rope to prevent the house from toppling over from strong winds.

One year, we had one of the worst typhoons I had experienced in my childhood. The ensuing flood engulfed our entire barrio, and it felt like our property was on an island in the middle of a big, dirty ocean. The floodwater was yellow from mountain run-off, and high waves lapped threateningly around our "island's" shores.

Since our house was situated on higher grounds than most of the others, we welcomed any of our friends and neighbors in need to stay with us for shelter.

Finding food in these conditions was nearly impossible. We were unable to fire up our clay stove to cook due to the damp conditions, so our menu consisted of raw rice and fruit - whatever we could find that was not contaminated by the floodwater.

After this flood raced through the barrios, it took a bit over two weeks for the rain to flash-wash away all the mud. Then, the pools were rendered down to puddles, and we were able to see the devastated roads and farm grounds again.

Everyone in our barrio, young and old, came together and cleaned up and repaired. Those who needed food were given food. Everyone who was able pitched in to rebuild or fortify houses that were damaged or destroyed by the floodwaters. Neighbors helping neighbors. Surely, this would not be the last storm, and knowing you were never alone in the worst of times was comforting and inspiring.

Dry Season

The dry season, from October to late-December, is when we harvested rice. Rice is the staple of all staples in the Filipino diet, so this was the most important task on the farm.

Rice stalks were cut by hand, and de-husking the rice meant pounding the grains with thick hardwood pestles (*bayo*) in large stone pots until the grains looked like the rice we commonly see sold in grocery stores. (This was the early 1940s to late 1950s, and rice mills were not used until the early 1960s.) The pounding was considered the most labor-intensive part and was often done in teams of two, each catching a rhythm as they took turns pounding the grains. I still remember the sound, like a drumbeat.

I cried often during this season, which reached temperatures as high as 110 degrees Fahrenheit. The heat did not cause as much pain as the stinging insects did. Large wasps seemed to target our lips, which would painfully swell up like donuts from their stings. Again, these fears were never excuses to discontinue working.

Notes for Context:

---

[1] Sunday is considered the day of the sabbath or the Lord's Day in Roman Catholicism. It's their day of rest - no work, no earning money.

Carabaos in action (top photo). The picture on the bottom left is a hardwood loom weaver similar to the one that my mother and sister used to weave fabric, and to the right is a photo of the resulting fabric from these weavers.

Work in the rice paddies.

Finding a rhythm while pounding the husks off the rice.

Chapter Three

Yielding from Our Yield

An important and exciting part of each season was the local open-air market. We were always sure to get to the market bright and early to set up our station to showcase our items, mainly corn, rice, and hogs.

The market was always lively and colorful, and getting to know the other regular vendors was a treat. Many of them were well-known for their specialties. Not only did we see a large variety of vegetables and fruit, but delicious street foods, including baked goods, such as mamon, pan de sal, and ensaymada; delicacies, like balut; sweets, like ube and halo-halo; too many to name[1]!

At the market, visitors witnessed how much Filipinos love food. We love to share food more than we love to eat it ourselves - sharing food is like our love language; it is how we show we care.

For our items, we either took payment in

pesos or bartered with other sellers or with people who sold commercial goods[2]. My mother used the money we made to purchase necessities that we were unable to make or grow ourselves. Hogs made the biggest profit, and this money went to our school tuition.

Sugar Cane Wine

Sugar cane was another major crop we grew on our farm. Harvest time for sugar cane was December to January. To process sugar cane after harvesting, we woke up early in the morning when the carabaos were most energetic. Their job was to pull an enormous wooden wheel, which was our sugar mill (*dadapilan*). This milling produced pure molasses.

We cooked (*anawang*) the molasses in an underground oven to burn off any impurities. We then dried this molasses, which produced a dark, grainy sugar. In a single season, the usual yield was about 100 gallons of sugar.

Another important product we made from sugar cane was a regional wine called basi. The juices from sugar cane were fermented using samac leaves and fruit, which gave the wine its characteristic color and flavor. We poured the basi wort into large earthen jars, covered the jars with paper or plastic, and left them alone in a dark room to ferment for three to nine months.

When it was time to harvest, we poured our basi into plastic or glass bottles - whatever bottle we could find that had an air-tight cover. The resulting wine was between 10-15% ABV. In a season, we produced 200-300 gallons of basi.

Notes for Context:

---

[1] mamon = tender spongecake

pan de sal = salty and slightly sweet bread

ensaymada = yeast bread rolled into a spiral, topped with room temperature butter, and dipped in sugar and sometimes shredded cheddar cheese

balut = boiled fertilized duck egg with usually embryo

ube = mashed and sweetened bright purple yam

halo-halo = shaved ice covered in variations of all sweets that Filipinos dream about, like sweet mung beans, ube, condensed milk, leche flan, coconut, ice cream, etc.

[2] The official currency of the Philippines is the Philippine Peso. Its ISO 4217 code is PHP, and it uses PHP or $ as its symbol. Peso coins are minted in the Security Plant Complex of the Philippines. At the time of this publishing (2023), they issued coins of one, five, ten, and 25 cents. Peso paper money or notes are printed at the Security Plant Complex or at the National Printing Office. Notes of 20, 50, 100, 200, 500, and 1,000 pesos are currently in circulation.

Boiling sugar. (above) Basi fermenting in clay pots. (below)

Chapter Four

Living and Learning

My oldest sister, Laureana, married a man named Epitacio Manzano before I started elementary school. They became like second parents to me, and they taught me how to read and write in English. I remember when they handed me my first book written in English. I had never seen anything like it in my life!

It was always a treat to read a magazine called *Bannawag* (which means "Dawn" in English[1]). Epitacio brought it home for us each week. At that time, this was the only English-language magazine available to us in our area, and it was published locally by Liwayway Publications, Inc. I remember feeling excited that I was actually able to read and understand the articles, even though it was old news - usually about a month old. The articles were about the goings-on around the Philippines and the world.

When we weren't reading, Epitacio brought me fishing and frogging. I learned so much from him, but sometimes, I was half asleep following him around on these long ventures.

May and June were the months in which he taught me how to forage for edible beetles (*abalabal*). Abalabal were salted and fried, boiled, or braised with vinegar.

Barefoot in Elementary School

Although neither of my parents was formally educated, they were highly emphatic about our academics. When I was seven years old, I started attending Bulbulala Elementary School.

My walk to school was six miles on a dirt road, and I got there barefoot. Since we had no backpacks, we either carried our books and supplies in our arms, or my father wove a bag (*bayon*) out of palm fronds for me. When it rained, we used umbrellas that were also hand-made out of palm. I was lucky to have relatives who lived close to the school, as they fed me during my lunch hour.

Unfortunately, World Word II had destroyed many of our country's schoolhouses between the years 1941-1946[2]. We were a poor region, and rebuilding infrastructure was incredibly slow or didn't happen at all. Our community had only one school building for grades one through four. We also used people's houses that were close to our campus as classrooms.

All we cared about was that we had a place to

gather that had large tables and enough chairs. About three years after I started school, the PTA received the funds to build two huts for grades five and six. These were bamboo and cogon huts with no flooring - just a few desks set on a dirt floor.

Grade school was a blur, but the teachers made much of it unforgettable. Mr. Banao, my fourth-grade teacher, was especially cruel. He asked students to solve problems on the board. If we were unable to solve them or were slow to answer, he grabbed our heads and knocked them against the board.

The upside to Mr. Banao was that he made all the teachers that followed seem like angels. My fifth-grade teacher, Miss Valeriana Afos, called me *kastila*, which means "Spanish," referring to my light skin color, as I had the lightest skin in the classroom. She never called me by my real name. I heard that she never married. My sixth-grade teacher was Mr. Andres Afos, who happened to be the cousin of my fifth-grade teacher, and he was just as nice and gentle with his students as she was.

Barefoot in Junior High School

Junior high school in the Philippines at that time was only a year long, and I cannot recollect much that is worth mentioning except for one brief moment that actually was not within school hours.

One afternoon, I was outside playing with my cousins and friends, as I normally did, when an older gentleman approached our group. He looked at me and called me over to him. He asked me to show him my palm. Although I was a bit apprehensive, I held out my hand. He grabbed it, faced my palm up, and squeezed it slightly so that the lines were a bit more pronounced. Squinting, he looked up at me and told me that he saw that I'd be going abroad in the future (*ballasiw ti taaw* in Ilocano).

I can't say I paid much attention to what he said at the time and thought it was just a silly thing. After all, I was only a poor farm boy digging in the dirt and mud. The only world I knew was my family, school, and our farm.

Still Barefoot in High School

After I finished junior high school, I did not wish to continue on to high school because my family was suffering financial hardship, and the high school was even further away from our home. I felt I needed to stay to help and did not want to be a burden.

My parents had something to say about that. They strongly encouraged me to keep going. I remember my father's exact words (translated from Ilocano), "Son, yes, we have a little property to care for here, but your education is something that will be retained within you, like the perfect inheritance that no one can ever take away from you." And finally, "Regret will come later."

Even though my parents didn't know how to read or write, they understood what it would take for their kids to succeed in life. They wanted more for us - they wanted us to be more than they ever were and to have more than they were ever able to provide for us. This selflessness was the greatest example of perfect, unconditional love. I wouldn't be where I am today if it was not for their sacrifice and vision for my future.

At that time, only a handful of high-ranking students were accepted into high school, and the campuses were very far from any of the barrios (also called districts or subdivisions outside of the municipalities). I felt that my acceptance into La Paz Catholic High School was "God's will."

Every day, I went from school to farm chores. On the days when it was extra busy on the farm, I copied my friends' homework to save time.

In high school, I felt especially blessed with a mentor named Mr. Nemsio Adrietico. He was my PE teacher, Preparatory Military Training (PMT) leader, basketball coach, and vocational teacher. He understood that I came from a poor family, so he donated his Pershing cap (a military-style cap that was part of the uniform) to me, amongst other things that were required that I could not otherwise afford. Such donations usually made me feel uncomfortable, but Mr. Adrietico put me to work to make me feel like I "earned" them. For example, he called me an officer of our PMT program, which kept me very busy[3].

The uniforms for PMT were a Gala Spanish style, and I was tasked with washing and ironing them. Ironing, especially, was not easy at that time. We used irons heated with charcoal, and I remember spending many weekends gathering and burning firewood to make charcoal to heat up the iron.

To get me out of the house, he brought me with him whenever there was an out-of-town basketball game, even though I was not a member of the team. I really enjoyed the hospitality and sites of the host towns.

One of the most negative memories I have of high school is the time I was involved in a feud with my entire barrio. It all started when I beat up a fellow student after he stole my vocational project. This caused the whole barrio to consider me an enemy. The tension was so high that I had to walk to school and back, holding a machete to protect myself.

One of my aunts owned a store next to our campus, and her son, my cousin, was intimidatingly huge, and he escorted me to and from campus. I had a temporary bodyguard.

This feud lasted for a whole month and only ended when my parents finally stepped in and reasoned with the family to settle the conflict, as it was getting tiresome, and it really was not completely my fault. I probably shouldn't have beaten him up, but he also should not have stolen a project I worked very hard to complete.

Notes for Context:

[1] The first issue of *Bannawag* was published and distributed on November 3, 1934, by Graphic Magazine. It was first conceived by Magdaleno A. Abaya of Candon, who had the idea to distribute an English-language magazine throughout the Ilocos region. This idea was first scoffed at by the then-owner-publisher, Graphic Magazine. It was eventually approved, on the condition that sales would be good and consistent. *Bannawag* has progressed with the times and continues its circulation throughout the Philippines as well as in other countries, such as Canada.

[2] The Philippines was ravaged by both American and Japanese forces during WWII between the years 1941 and 1946. So much of the infrastructure – places of business, schools, homes, and other structures – was bombed and burned, and the country was rendered unrecognizable, as were the people. Approximately one million Filipinos, soldiers and civilians, were killed,

especially toward the end, during the final push by the Japanese.

[3] At the time, Preparatory Military Training (PMT) was required for high school students. This originated in 1936, under President Quezon, under the provisions of Article VII Title III of the National Defense Act. Preparatory Military Training was required for students attending all public and private schools.

My Preparatory Military Training (PMT) portrait

Chapter Five

Leaving the Nest

My sisters were the managers of the family. They took the lead and helped all of us work together harmoniously to get through each day successfully, whether we were working outside in the fields or in our house trying to get along in our small space. Their care and life lessons did not leave me even when all of us went our separate ways.

My first sister was the first to leave the family to start one of her own just before I entered elementary school, as I had mentioned earlier. My second oldest sister, Aurelia, moved to the big city, Manila, in late-1956 and found a good job with a company called Philippine-American Embroidery. This was a relief for the family, as it meant one less tuition bill.

My older brother was the first to graduate from high school. He moved to Manila and became a manager for a lumpia wrapper manufacturing company. My younger brother continued working with me on the farm. After he graduated in 1963, however, he moved to Manila and became a mechanic.

My parents remained in Abra. Although I often missed them, I could not visit as often as I'd wished because it was too expensive to travel. To our relief, my eldest sister stayed in Abra, and she and her husband took care of my parents and helped them tend their farm.

Life as a Squatter

I felt lost after graduating from high school. Deflated and lacking a sense of direction, I caught myself pondering, "What is the purpose of my existence?"

My history teacher, Mr. Martinez, noticed my distress. He sat me down and began with, "Seek to find and do not yield." This reminded me of the gospel of Matthew 7:7-8: "Ask, and it will be given to you; seek, and you will find it; knock on the door, and it will open for you." He ended with: "You live here in a very remote area. Go to Manila, the big city."

Everyone seemed to move to the already-overpopulated city of Manila. Some are never heard from again. Others, you hear about from community members. I watched my siblings find decent jobs when they made the big move to the city, but I had so much doubt in myself. I couldn't imagine anyone would hire me for anything. But I thought that if I didn't move forward, I was already choosing failure.

So, the beginning of my path was defined for me; with some deliberation, I finally made the move.

When I arrived in Manila, just as I feared, I had absolutely no luck finding a job. Luckily, a cousin in town owned a barber shop on G Tuazon Street in Sampaloc, Manila, and he trained me to cut hair. After six months of working as a barber, they promised to help me get into college. That is, until I was stricken with the flu. My illness was so severe that I had to move back home to the family farm in Abra indefinitely.

It was the beginning of January 1962. Nearly half of a year had passed, another harvest cycle was completed, and I couldn't get Mr. Martinez's words out of my head. I convinced myself to give Manila another go. This time, I found a job right off the bat as a security guard with First Security Inc.

First Security gave me a recommendation that helped me get my foot in the door at their headquarters, and they gave me my first assignment at Main Prudential Bank at Plaza Goity. This was such a boost and I felt so proud of myself. I felt like I was actually going to do this city life thing; if I could keep this pace, I'd be able to stay in Manila for at least three more years.

City living still proved to be expensive, and my oldest brother and I lived as squatters in Tondo, Manila. Our barong-barong was infested with rats and cockroaches, and the mosquito population was the worst I had ever experienced[1].

Tondo, at the time, was also known for having one of the highest crime rates in Manila. Whenever I was assigned night duty, I slept at the bank and went home in the morning to avoid being mugged, or worse, by gangsters.

This is how I lived for three years. My luck and life changed when I turned in an application at the US Naval Recruiting Center in Sangley Point, Cavite City, Philippines.

A few months had passed since turning in the application and I almost forgot about it. Finally, I received an invitation in the mail to take the written and physical exams. After learning that I had passed these exams, I was one of the fortunate men to be offered an opportunity to join the United States Navy[2]. While my brother moved to another safer city, I was eagerly waiting to begin my new career.

Notes for Context:

[1] Per the Philippine Statistics Authority, a squatter is "one who settles on the land of another or without the owner's consent, whether in urban or rural areas." When land was abandoned in urban areas, such as Davao City, Manila, after WWII, most of this land became crowded with make-shift housing called barong-barong. Shelters were made from salvaged material, such as scrap lumber, flattened cans, billboards, cartons, and bottles. No water, electricity, and sewage were provided. Groups of barong-barong are considered "slums."

[2] Filipinos were recruited into the US Navy (USN) beginning in 1901 when President McKinley signed an executive order allowing the USN to enlist Filipinos for insular services. They were limited to steward duties until 1946. One of the lures to joining the USN was the Nationality Act of 1940, in which aliens who served honorably in the armed forces for three years or more could be naturalized as US citizens and granted permanent residence. This also applied to their spouses and dependents.

My siblings and I as adults.
Top: Prisco (youngest), Me (4th), Emiliano (3rd).
Bottom: Laureana (eldest), Aurelia (2nd)

Chapter Six

From Russia with Love

Just before I was sworn into the Navy, I met **a girl named Elisa Carreon.** She liked to simply be called Lisa. I often visited my God sister, Candy Tagura, at her company, Fil-Amlife Homes, in Quezon City.

Lisa just happened to live across the street from Candy's office and was close friends with her. I saw Lisa every time I visited her and was actually surprised that she always wanted to come out with us, even when we visited Candy's sister in a neighboring city.

After a few of these visits, I remember suddenly realizing how pretty Lisa was. Thereafter, I felt stunned to the point to where I was barely able to say a word around her. I never felt that way around anyone before and didn't know what was happening. Luckily, she was very good at filling in the awkward pauses, as she talked a lot and also talked very fast.

One day, I got up the courage to ask her out without Candy. On a warm October evening (1964), we watched "From Russia with Love" at the Odeon Theater in Manila. The evening felt special – she looked so beautiful that night and I don't think anyone ever made me laugh so much. A couple of things bothered me, though – I have to admit I wasn't completely honest with her, as I was too embarrassed to tell her that I was living as a squatter and was not sure how or when to tell her that I was in the process of joining the Navy.

Since the Navy meant that I had to leave for months at a time, I knew I needed to have the conversation with her before flying out to the United States. I was haunted by the hurt look on her face, but I was sure to tell her that I'd miss her and would be in touch.

In the Navy

While traveling to America was sought after and exciting for many, my first trip overseas was probably one of the saddest times in my life, as I thought that my last date with Lisa would also be the last time I would ever see her again.

However, I snapped out of it and focused when I learned that I was assigned to the San Diego Naval Training Center to become a Seabee. Each day after boot camp, along with other Filipino trainees, I was sent to stewards training, where we learned cooking techniques and the proper etiquette for serving the officers.

These were not glamorous tasks by any means,

but we didn't seem to have a choice at the time. We were told by the officers that having Filipinos and black Americans cook for and serve the officers had been a "tradition" since the very beginning. None of us really knew any better, and even if we did, what could we do?

The first official duty station I was ordered to was Quonset Naval Station, Rhode Island. Here, I was attached to the VS 22 Submarine Hunter Squadron on a three-year tour. We worked aboard the USS Saratoga, the USS Lake Champlain, and the USS Essex aircraft carriers. My squadron's main job was to pick up astronauts who had landed on the sea.

Working on aircraft carriers was quite an adjustment, and seasickness got the best of me too often. My main job on the carriers was to clean the state rooms of the officers. We also served as stewards in the officers' wardrooms after meals. I was young, clumsy, and unsure, but fortunately, the first person they paired me with was a very kind, older Filipino who taught me how to stay out of trouble every step of the way.

I learned the hierarchy quickly, and it was important to know and stick to our place, which, as you can imagine, was incredibly nerve-racking. I remember one particular special event I helped with.

The officers were dressed in their formal white uniforms. One of the dishes we served was split pea soup. I took extra care to stay on-point, but this made things worse, and my hands shook every time I poured this bright green soup near these stark white suits.

Of course, I inevitably spilled on an officer's

shoulder. I cowered and apologized profusely, "I'm sorry, Sir. I didn't mean it." He got up and yelled, "Oh!! Is it hot?" and he looked like he was going to hurt me, but as I cowered, he simply wiped himself off and sat back down, shaking his head. His response could have been much worse, but I thought he probably wanted to keep the rest of his whites clean.

Another time, I was paired with a Filipino man of a higher rank than me. We were working at a table and he had me do all of our tasks while he sat back and teased me. I tried to stay calm and professional, but a fire was smoldering inside of me. After we finished for the night, we were sent back to our quarters, but I decided I needed to get that feeling off my chest right then and there. I called him into the passageway and immediately threw one punch after another.

Passersby finally pulled me back. His face was bloody, and he was immediately escorted to sickbay. As punishment, I was restricted to my quarters, unable to go out for 24 hours. It could have been a worse punishment, but they concluded after hearing testimonies from witnesses that I was retaliating against his bullying, and what I did was somehow justifiable.

One night, as I sat staring at the wall in my sleeping quarters, I decided to write Lisa a letter. I detailed my adventures, the good and ugly ones, and couldn't help but tell her that I was thinking about her, even if I risked scaring her away. A few weeks passed, and my overall mood changed when I received my first letter from her!

Homeport Foolishness

Whenever we were sent back to our homeport, we immediately reported to the Bachelors Officers Quarters (BOQ). From there, we continued our service to the officers in the wardrooms and cleaned their staterooms five days a week and some weekends.

When we weren't working, we often went off-base to explore and decompress. One memory of this was the night my friend Jojo and I went out to downtown Providence. We were drawn to the bright lights of a particular bar. Once we stepped through the doors, the music was deafening, the air was smoky, and the dance floor was populated with hoards of ladies drinking, dancing, and having a good time.

We joined in on the fun and bought rounds of drinks. The women were so friendly and happy. Halfway through the night, we blinked a few times and noticed that many of the ladies were kissing ... each other. Jojo and I looked at each other, made sure we paid up, and left. This was the first time I had encountered a gay bar.

After three years, I was transferred to the U.S. Naval Mobile Battalion, and here, the other Filipinos that I mixed with were unusually mischievous.

One night, a group of five of us were having fun drinking beer at the Enlisted Club (EM). A guy in our group from Bicol, Philippines - a known troublemaker - was watching a very intoxicated Caucasian man who was shouting and grabbing drinks off of other sailors' tables. The troublemaker declared that when this man left the bar, he'd ambush him. After this pummeling, all of us immediately sprinted to our quarters. We soon heard a commotion within the base and were told that our base's security forces were looking for five Filipino sailors. I don't think I slept a wink that night.

The next day, all Filipinos on base were asked to line up, and then they called the victim over. As he stood in front of us, I noticed that the poor man had stitches all over his face. The Chief Master at Arms asked him to identify the person who did that to him and to point out everyone involved. With a smug look on his stitched-up face, he said, "I don't know - they all look alike." I swallowed this insult and called it good since none of us suffered consequences.

Bootcamp - 1964

Chapter Seven

Da Nang

On July 9, 1968, I reported to the 12th NCR in Davisville, Rhode Island, for further military training by the Marine Corps Tactical Military Combat Operations. Shortly after, my Naval Mobile Construction Battalion One (MCB-1) deployed to Da Nang, Vietnam.

A couple of months had passed in Vietnam, when I gained a new-found respect for my fellow comrades, the higher ranks, and our mission. I felt the loss of fellow Seabee, Lieutenant Junior Grade (LTJG) Arthur David Moscrip, Jr., may he Rest in Peace. LTJG Moscrip was a commander of my Battalion, MCB-1, and was killed when his jeep hit a land mine. He was a young 25 years old.

More news of fallen soldiers became too common, such as Master Chief Smith, who was also in my Battalion and I remember running across a few times. These are two of 85 Seabees who gave their lives while serving our country in Vietnam. I felt a soreness in my chest as I imagined their families receiving the call and letter.

Even though the US is not my homeland, I felt a strong loyalty for my new home; I was placed there to keep my country's democracy safe, which meant stopping the spread of communism.

It is our, as it is for all of the branches of the United States Military, to serve and protect the citizens of the United States of America, no matter the risk, in order to allow every single American Citizen to continue on with their lives in freedom. This is why I am here; this is why WE are here. God, give us strength to be steadfast in our mission.

We continued to serve our Battalion officers. We picked up their food from the mess hall, and after every meal, we cleaned the wardroom and hand-washed dishes and silverware because a scullery machine was not available for us. But this time, with more of an understanding of the pressures that they and all of us were under.

Whenever it was my turn for guard duty, I stood at the checkpoint fully armed with sidearms and M-16 rifles and a renewed spirit. During the day, I went back to cleaning the officers' huts.

One day, during a lunch break, I noticed a flyer that was lying on a table near me as I was sipping a cup of broth. My eyes widened as I read through a list of new options available for Filipinos who held the Steward rating. I wasn't sure if I was reading a tabloid[1].

Yes, all roles were important, but I was feeling complacent. Each day, I felt like I was just going through the motions. I had an undeniable pull to be more useful but had no clue what to do about it or if these were just pipe dreams.

Finally, one of the positions caught my eye. A few days later, I walked into our administrative office and requested a change to my government rating. It wasn't long before I was notified about my acceptance to train to become a Naval Construction Electrician. This felt right.

Notes for Context:

[1]After 1946, Filipinos were recruited per agreement with the Republic of the Philippines and Article XXVII of the Military Bases Agreement. The rising need for stewards to serve the US officers increased, and an agreement was negotiated in 1952 that allowed 1,000 Filipino citizens to be enlisted each year; this number grew to 2,000 soon after.

The inequities between recruits in the Navy came to light in the early 1960s. Filipinos, in particular, being predominant in the Steward rating was challenged. It wasn't until February of 1971 that Philippine nationals were allowed to be recruited as Seamen Recruits Vice Stewardsman, which gave them a broader range of Navy rating options.

Furthermore, in 1972, the Application Qualification Test (AQT) was implemented for the pre-enlistment screening of Filipino applicants, replacing the Philippine Application Test (PAT), which only allowed them a Steward rating. The AQT opened up more opportunities for Filipinos, such as for Aviation Boatswain's Mate (AB), Aviation Machinist's Mate (AD), Boilerman (BT), and Machine Repairman (MM).

The Steward rating was completely discontinued by December 1974. Members of the former Steward rating were merged with members of the Commissary rating in January 1975 to form the new Mess Management Specialist (MS) rating.

(Cover Photo) 7R Vietnam - 1968-1969

Chapter Eight

Absence Makes the Heart Grow Fonder

On October 26, 1968, I used my **R & R leave to fly home to the Philippines and to Lisa.** She was my pen pal for four years, and when we were finally reunited, it felt like we had never parted.

It was the second day of the trip. I walked over to her house and was shown to her bedroom door by her parents. Her door was closed since she was getting ready for our night out. I don't even know how long I stood nervously staring at her door before I finally knocked. The second it opened, I grabbed her hand, kissed her, and asked her if she would marry me.

Without hesitation and with tears in her eyes, she said *yes*.

Since I was on leave throughout our relationship, I had only heard about her family members through letters. So, the next important step for Lisa was for her to introduce me to all of them in person!

I was welcomed with open arms by most of her family on October 28, 1968. First, I met her oldest brother, Ariston, Jr. Next was her oldest sister, Ate' Nene and Ate' Nene's husband, Kuya Joe. Kuya Joe took us to the Municipal Court of Meycauayan, Bulacan, for our formal engagement[1].

After this special R & R, I was sent back to Vietnam. Lisa contacted me once I reached my command and she was upset because her uncle Pepe, whom I had not yet met, was enraged when he learned of our engagement. She was his favorite niece, and this news put him in an alcoholic rage. Luckily, she was able to talk him down and get his blessings. He, in fact, ended up becoming our primary sponsor and played the piano for our wedding.

Going to the Chapel

It was the end of January 1969, and we completed our Battalion's deployment in Vietnam. I had served in the war zone for nine months and thanked the Lord that I survived. I then put in my request to return home to the Philippines for a very personal mission.

When I arrived, I sat down to look at the laundry list of tasks I thought I needed to help Lisa complete. I was amazed to see that everything, from sending out invitations to booking the venue, had been done by Lisa. A restaurant was booked for our rehearsal dinner, and our sponsors were prepared with their duties and items. Lisa was very busy.

Our sponsors were highly regarded citizens of the community. We had professors from the University of the Philippines, such as Professor Jose V. Carreon, Professor Norma E. Noriega, and Mrs. Cecillia G. Carlos. Also, Pedro T. Carreon, the former mayor of Meycauayan, Bulacan, was one of our sponsors[2].

Before the day of the ceremony, we received a Sacrament of Penance as a puritanical of the Catholic faith[3].

Then the day finally arrived. February 8, 1969, has gone down in history as the happiest day of my life. This is the day that Lisa and I tearfully and joyfully exchanged our vows under the blessed eaves of Saint Rita Catholic Church in Quezon City.

Nearly the entire Carreon family was in attendance. The only ones missing were the Arsenio family. As I watched Lisa interact with her family, I noticed that Lisa was considered the "darling" of the Carreon family. She was treated like royalty, and everyone loved and fussed over her.

The attendees on my side of the family who were able to attend included my mother, Venancia; my two brothers, Emiliano and Prisco; and my nephew, Nicanor. As representatives of the Abo family, they made sure Lisa and I knew and felt that we had the entire family's blessings and support.

After the ceremony, we held a large, extravagant reception at the Aristocrat Restaurant in Quezon City. The chef also made a fancy, delicious wedding cake, which was chocolate with white frosting. Our guests were treated to amazing food.

Dancing, toasts, prayers, and so many heartfelt hugs. I remember feeling our guests' happiness and love surrounding us like an energy field.

For our honeymoon, we stayed in the Ambassador Hotel in Baguio City[4]. The newlywed weeks that followed were such a dizzying whirlwind. There were moments when I glanced over at my sweet Lisa, and the whirlwind stopped briefly. And I felt deep within my heart true love's bliss. I felt forever.

Notes for Context:

[1]Kuya (pronounced koo-yah) means big brother; Ate' (pronounced ah'teh) means big sister.

[2]The party of sponsors, usually aunts, uncles, and extended family members, is an important part of Filipino Catholic wedding ceremonies. Secondary sponsors include the coin, veil, cord, and candle sponsors, who bring the corresponding articles and partake in the wedding rituals surrounding these items during the usually very long, elaborate wedding ceremony.

[3]In the Catholic faith, the Sacrament of Penance, as a puritanical Catholic faith, is a confession   session to be granted forgiveness for sins committed after baptism.

[4]Baguio City, located in Benguet of Northern Luzon, Philippines, was known for its beautiful botanical gardens and is now a resort town and a popular tourist destination in the Philippines.

February 8, 1969

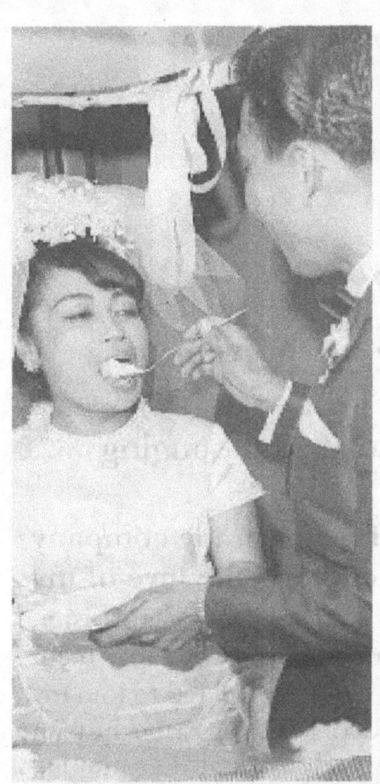

Chapter Nine

Deployment, Love, and Longing

After 30 days of being in the company of my best friend and the love of my life, I had to leave again. Lisa's sister, Aurora, kept her company in our apartment in Meycauayan, Bulacan, as I was ordered to join my new Battalion in Puerto Rico. I can't describe the pain I felt in my heart and stomach as I left my stunning new bride.

I joined my new Battalion, MCB-71. We built several structures near Roosevelt Road, including Camp Moscrip, dedicated to LTJG Moscrip. As mentioned earlier, LTJG Moscrip lost his life defending our country in Vietnam.

After a few months in Puerto Rico, I received some special news: My daughter, Analiz, was born on October 14, 1969. Becoming a father made my heart grow to immense proportions. I told everyone in earshot about it.

Then, a sobering reality set in. I was not with

my wife at the hospital to allow her to squeeze my hand until it turned purple while she was going through labor pains. I wasn't in the room to cut the umbilical cord. What if something went wrong with Lisa or the baby? And the thought of the number of people embracing my first child before I am able to. While Lisa never expressed disappointment, I felt it for both of us.

Missing out on milestones such as this is part of being in the active military. Do we ever become numb to this? Is it simply duty first? - A mental and physical agreement? Simply protocol? Do we agree to not feel?

I can say at that point in time, I was not there yet; I should have been at the hospital with my family.

Eight months later, a team and I were deployed to Guantanamo Bay, Cuba. Here, I was assigned as Electrical Leader in Crew Detail at the Camp Barkeley Marine Barracks. Our missions were to build 18 portables and the Butler Building, and to install the interior wiring in all.

On April 25, 1971, upon completion of our deployment, I decided to re-enlist as a Construction Electrician Third Class Petty Officer. Lt. Lucas administered the oath once I was accepted. This promotion gave me a $6,000 bonus[1].

Soon after, I was scheduled for shore duty, and when I contacted my detailer, he told me that they were sending me to the Naval Communication Station in Honolulu, Hawaii, with an accompanying tour.

This was the perfect time and place to bring Lisa and my new daughter to the United States of

America. I was granted permission to go back to the Philippines to bring Lisa and Analiz with me on my next tour.

Meeting my first daughter for the first time was surreal, magical, and emotional. The touch of her hand gave me yet another inspiration.

Immediately after I arrived, the three of us were processed at the U.S. Naval Base in Sangley Point, Cavite City, Philippines. We left the Philippines in May of 1971 on an aircraft from Clark Air Force Base, Pampanga, Philippines[2].

We heard that the day after we had left, a bank inside the base had been robbed, and a Marine lieutenant was killed. When such tragedies happen, the whole base is on Red Alert and shuts down. This definitely would have been a hurdle for our departure. We felt lucky to have left when we did.

Notes for Context:

[1] $6,000 is equivalent to $60,000-$70,000 at the time of publishing.

[2] At that time, passports were not required for dependents to travel.

This was written on the back of the above photo.

Barracks in the background.

Chapter Ten

First Steps on American Soil

Lisa and Analiz's first steps in the US were in Rhode Island. We stayed in the Navy Lodge for a month, awaiting my order to Honolulu, Hawaii, to be processed.

This was a great opportunity to explore Rhode Island. We strolled around Providence City, Boston Park, and Chinatown. As we explored, we shopped! We bought a brand new burgundy 1971 Pontiac Lemans and furniture to ship to Hawaii.

One activity I could not give up was fishing. I asked around for the best places on base to cast out. Perch and eel were abundant, and we were able to share our catch with our new-found friends.

Lisa made many new friends, such as the manager of the Navy Lodge, Mrs. Ricario. They became Mahjong buddies.

While here, we checked out the neighboring states of New York and New Jersey with my friend,

Bobby Datan, who was a Seabee Engineer. All of us explored the Rockefeller Center, the Empire State Building, and Chinatown.

On July 28, 1971, Lisa, Analiz, and I started our cross-country journey. This trek took three days and three nights. We drove 16 hours each day, stopping only for diaper changes at rest areas, and stayed at motels enroute.

We finally reached Oakland, California, and decided to check in at the very friendly-looking Aloha Hotel. We felt lucky - night was approaching, and we were growing tired of seeing "NO VACANCY" signs.

When we checked in, two men next door approached us. They were kind and enthusiastic and offered candy to Analiz. The next day, we were given directions to the US Army Depot, where they shipped cars to Honolulu, Hawaii. We brought our car there for shipment and were soon on our way to Travis Airforce Base.

We landed at Honolulu International Airport and stepped off the plane into hot, humid air that was fragrant with plumeria. We heard live ukulele music and the iconic voices of Don Ho or Elvis Presley everywhere we walked.

My sponsor picked us up and brought us to our hotel, reserved for us as Temporary Lodging Allowance (TLA). We stayed in the TLA until we found a home.

We met many people in Honolulu. 'Manang' Marina Gabertan and her family were very kind, and we visited them almost every weekend. They loved to play with and babysit our daughter.

They introduced us to other families who moved there from the Philippines at gatherings. These took place in people's homes, at parks, and on beaches. Talking, laughing, and plenty of food.

Lisa was incredible. Everyone talked to her like they had known her all their lives. It was impressive watching her social skills in action and seeing her so happy. We probably wouldn't have gotten to know so many people if it wasn't for her. I began to feel a strong sense of belonging with this community - this mix of Filipinos and Hawaiians.

I discovered that I wasn't so bad at socializing myself and made my share of friends during this time. I became particularly close to a fellow Seabee named Rene Angeles and his family at Barbers Point Naval Air Station. His son, Munching, was about the same age as Analiz, and we enjoyed many Filipino and Hawaiian gatherings together. We were both Ilocano and had similar tempers and senses of humor, so we shared many laughs together.

Rene's wife, Norma, and Lisa became close, as well, although their personalities were opposite, with Norma being the quiet one. When their daughter, Kimberly, was born, they selected me as her *Ninong* or Godfather[1]. Kimberly and I still have a close, inseparable connection to this day.

Notes for Context:

---

[1] In the Filipino culture, parents choose anywhere from one to 20 Godparents - usually couples for their soon-to-be-born child. The Godparents attend the baptism and are expected to give gifts for birthdays and other milestones. The Godfather is called "ninong" and the Godmother is "ninang."

A Filipino gathering with friends in Hawaii.

Lisa and Norma with Analiz and Munching.

Adults can teeter-totter, too! Lisa (right) and Norma in Hawaii.

Chapter Eleven

A Growing Family

Jennifer was born on April 3, 1973, at Tripler Army Hospital, Honolulu, Hawaii.

Just a year and a half later, we welcomed our third daughter, Evangeline. We held their baptismal parties at Manang Marina's house.

Immediately after Evangeline's birth, we started to feel the mental and financial challenges of adjusting to a new country while parenting three children.

Lisa continued to amaze me in so many ways; she was able to adapt to the simple life despite growing up around wealth. Dealing with finances seemed to be one of Lisa's many strong points, as she was always conscious of our expenses. Most importantly, she taught me to always be satisfied with whatever we had and to not be envious of those around us.

In spite of this, I felt that we needed more

money to support our family of now five, and I often searched for odd jobs to do around the community. I took a part-time job at the MWR Auto Hobby Shop, was a movie operator, installed outdoor lights at residences, and helped out as a ranch hand on a Portuguese ranch[1].

I found the ranch hand job most interesting, where I maintained the motors for their hoist. I appreciated the peace and quiet of the ranch. Also, the smell of the field and livestock reminded me of my family's home back in Abra.

The most valuable benefit to me besides money? Whenever the owner butchered a cow, he gave me scrap meat, the innards, heads, and feet, most of which are not exactly in high demand but were parts I believe many people who do not know any better miss out on.

When growing up in the Philippines, there was hardly any waste of any part of an animal. Filipinos have mastered ways to cook virtually every digestible part of an animal, and it is always delicious. I shared this "animal part" wealth with other members of our Filipino community, who were always so grateful.

For my first assignment for my Battalion, I was sent to our Radio Transmitting Facility at Lualualei, Hawaii, as a safety inspector. I was also in charge of repairing all motors for the radio facilities, streetlights with a bucket track, and the radio tower. It took 2.1 megawatts to run our radio facility tower. We maintained four generators, each 100 kilowatts, and each month, a big task was to test-run them.

After five years in Hawaii, I was given the order to attend a 32-week training at a technical school at Fort Gordon in Augusta, Georgia. I attended the Army Signal School for Telephone Technicians (Telephone Exchange Dial Central Office) to learn the skills required for my next assignment.

While there, I further practiced my wife's social skills and ended up making many Army friends. There were 12 lakes within the army base, and I was able to fish at every one of them on weekends with my new friends. We enjoyed our catch at picnics around the lakes.

Upon completion of my training in Georgia, I was awarded a Navy Enlisted Classification Code (CE-5642 or Central Office Exchange Technician). Following that, I received an order to travel to Keflavik, Iceland, on an accompanying tour.

Land of the Midnight Sun

I spent the next three years in Keflavik for my tour of duty. Here, I was in charge of telephone communications with four Icelandic operators and two Icelandic technicians. My team maintained both interior and exterior telephone lines, including close-circuit TV cables (CCTV).

On August 10, 1979, I was sent to the NAVFAC Technical Training Center in Norfolk, Virginia, to take a three-week course on intrusion alarm systems, system design theory, maintenance, and operations.

I was in charge of their base alarm system and trained crews on installation, troubleshooting, and maintenance. Also, whenever a new Filipino family came to Keflavik, my office was called to hook up their residential telephone lines to ease the potential language barrier.

While heading base security, we only ran across some minor offenses, such as catching shoplifters at the Navy Exchange. I had night duty as the Public Works Duty Officer (PWDO), managed our electrical crews and utilities (plumbing and builders), and maintained base station emergencies after workdays.

We didn't get many emergency calls from residents during the day because public works civilians didn't have any work orders; they basically spent their time drinking coffee and chatting all day. I needed more to do, so I got a part-time job maintaining slot machines at the BOQ.

My family seemed to have adjusted well to our new surroundings, even though the climate was the extreme opposite of what we were used to in Hawaii and our country of origin.

We explored several social clubs that were available to us. One of the clubs that we especially enjoyed was the Filipino-American Association. They offered many recreational activities for members, like bingo and slot machines. And of course, we made many friends through this club, which made our stay here so much nicer.

We found the Icelandic locals to be very kind and generous. We got to know the people who worked at the local fishery. Whenever we visited, they encouraged us to bring a plastic bag so that they could fill it with fish for no charge.

A Monster Sighting

On Lisa and I's way to Germany to begin a five-day R & R, our airplane had to turn back around to Keflavik due to a hydraulic leak in one of our plane's engines. Our new flight ended up being diverted to Scotland due to snowstorms.

One day, while exploring Scotland, we passed a large crowd of photographers with tripods all along the banks of the Loch Ness. We were told that there was a monster sighting recently, and everyone was waiting for an opportunity to see it for themselves; I heard later that it never "reappeared."

We ended up stuck in Scotland for over a week. In fact, we thought we were waiting for a new aircraft to head to Germany, but instead, for some reason, they wanted to repair the one that had broken down. If we had waited for that, by the time the repaired aircraft arrived, my R & R would have expired. We figured that Germany wasn't meant to be for us at that time.

Since we were in this other country, we decided to take full advantage of our time there. We got to know the warm, hospitable Scottish people. They encouraged us to try their interesting national dish called haggis. We were almost sad when we were told it was safe enough to go back to Keflavik.

I became very close to the people in the Flight Operations Department in Keflavik since my team maintained their RED phones (hotline) and had to work with them regularly. Whenever there were available R & R flights going to Germany and other places in Europe, I was the first to know.

Notes for Context:

[1] Around 1880, as the demand for sugar grew, sugar plantations were in need of workers since Western diseases had decimated most of the local Hawaiian workers. Nearly 25,000 Portuguese laborers migrated to Hawaii to fill this need. Of course, the Portuguese influence remains a large part of the beautiful Hawaiian culture. Good examples of their influence are Portuguese sausage, found on most menus when you visit Hawaii, and the ukulele.

That one time, our flight got diverted to Scotland ...

Lisa stands in front of a replica of "Nessy."

Chapter Twelve

"Icelandic the Terrible"

On January 24, 1979, the girls, Lisa and I welcomed our last-born and only son, Joel, a.k.a., "Icelandic the Terrible" (ha, ha). He is also the only family member with two birth certificates: Icelandic and American. Joel was baptized on St. Patrick's Day of that same year.

On September 1, 1980, when Joel was a year and eight months old, I was sent to shore duty with the U.S. Naval Mobile Battalion 14 in Jacksonville, Florida, to maintain the Battalion's facility.

This tour required plenty of odd jobs. I was put in charge of the reserve personnel's projects and training coordination at Camp Blanding National Army Reserve and School; was coordinator for the reserve officers for their quarters in the BOQ; coordinated with the NAS supply officers for their meals in the mess hall; picked up personnel from legal holds at the Base Master at Arms to work for our Battalion's compound; was the senior chief's assistant, who managed personnel records; and was a storekeeper. My favorite task of all was coordinating the annual Seabee Ball, as it provided a creative outlet for me[1].

After my four years in the Land of Fire and Ice, I was given a one-year unaccompanied order to Souda Bay, Crete, Greece. Here, I maintained all telephone exchanges, including commercial lines and auto von lines, as well as all communications with the Army Headquarters (NAMFI) NATO missile firing installation. I was under the Detachment of Communications (Ashore and Afloat) at Souda Bay and maintained the Dial Central Office and all outside telephone lines. My detachment included electronic technicians and radiomen, a radioman chief, and an OIC named Lt. Smith.

I met some wonderful locals, and they really knew how to party. One of my new Greek friends had invited me to a gathering he was hosting. He apparently was from a wealthy background, and I was treated like an ambassador at the party. Everyone at the party called me "Mr. Joe." No one ever called me "Mr. Joe" before! I think I smiled from ear to ear each time I heard that.

Toward the end of the night, the adults played a game in which everyone stacked five dishes on top of each other, and after placing the last one, they made everyone drink wine. Oh, what an experience that was! As you can imagine, not many sober partygoers were left by the night's end.

Speaking of drinking, our base only had one

small bar, and the manager of our Navy Exchange, who happened to be a friend of mine, asked me to bartend. I told him that I had no experience mixing drinks, and he told me not to worry - that I'd be a "pro" in a night or two.

After my first couple of nights of bartending, I learned that he was kind of right. I wasn't quite a "pro," but our customers were mainly from the US Army's NATO Headquarters, and they always requested that I make their drinks a "double," and they ended up getting drunk too quickly to notice that I didn't know what the heck I was doing. I held this odd but interesting job for 11 months.

Our division often went out to eat in the surrounding villages and we always looked for steak on the menu. The only seasonings the restaurants used on meat here were olive oil, salt, and lemon, which I thought was rather bland, but everyone else seemed to like it that way.

There is nothing like the beautiful, clear-water coast of Greece. When I strolled around the downtown area, I was amazed at their sophisticated sculptures and their buildings' incredible, unique architecture.

Notes for Context:

[1] The first Seabee Ball was held in 1943 in Port Hueneme, California, to commemorate the founding of the Seabees. Traditionally, it is a very formal event, with the ladies dressed in floor-length ball gowns and the officers dressed in uniform, the youngest and the oldest Seabees are recognized in the ceremony, a king and queen are chosen, and there is a cake cutting, followed by singing "The Song of the Seabees."

Lisa and I at the Seabee Ball in Keflavik, Iceland (1978).

Seabee Ball with friends.

❧ ・ ☙

Chapter Thirteen

A Lifelong Vacation Earned

After a year in Greece, on October 2, 1985, I received a call from my detailer. To my surprise, he asked me if I was ready to retire. I didn't have to contemplate too long to give him my answer, "Yes."

I was offered an accompanying duty to the Naval Station in Guantanamo, Cuba, where I had a billet of my Navy Enlisted Classification (NEC) 5642. Once I received my order, I was on my way and sent for my family as soon as housing became available.

On November 2, 1985, I reported to the Public Works Department. Instead of working on my NEC Code, I was ordered to manage four shops: Electric, carpenter, plumbing, and metal trade. My supervisors were a division Chief and Chief Warrant Officer Geiger, and I was assigned a secretary to help with typing up our division's input and output reports, including the evaluations of our crew.

I enjoyed leading the Physical Training (PT)

drills, which were held each Monday. Once a month, we held 5k races. The competition was fierce because if the participants beat their own personal best, they were rewarded by being exempted for two months. The energy was always electric during these runs; everyone was highly motivated, and a vast majority were indeed rewarded.

My management duties seemed endless. I loved it. I was responsible for all priority work orders, represented my division at meetings, and as Division Counselor, I was regularly briefed by the Base Counselor on any new Department of Defense rules and regulations. I was also honored with the responsibility of informing retiring Seabee personnel of their benefits. This is where I felt all of my work came full circle.

As the Public Works Duty Officer (PWDO), I oversaw the resolution of all emergencies that came into our office. I was also the Station Duty Officer (SDO), which gave me an opportunity to watch our whole station participate in defensive exercises.

Defensive exercises were as practical as they were entertaining - they simulated evacuations using dependents who volunteered to ride in a Cl30 Aircraft for a week.

The most intense moments of these defensive exercises occurred when we simulated squad patrol, which was an overnight exercise. All participants were required to wear full combat gear, and blanks were used for ammunition. For sustenance, we practiced consuming MREs (Meals Ready to Eat)[1].

During our off-hours, I spent time with my family and friends. We enjoyed different activities with the Fil-Am (Filipino-American) Club. On base, we had an annual Naval Station Carnival, the Seabee Ball, and Knights of Columbus parties. Almost every weekend, when the weather cooperated, we picnicked on the beach. They also offered dependents cruises and helicopter rides.

Christmas was very special here, as we held huge holiday potlucks. Attendees contributed their special traditional cultural dishes. Since we had quite a diverse group, the table was always full of incredible dishes that I probably would never have tasted if it wasn't for these parties.

The base in Guantanamo Bay, Cuba, provided so many unique opportunities for our family. One that we were sure to take advantage of was scuba diving groups, and our daughters, Analiz, Jennifer, and Evangeline, became Certified Open Water Divers.

A Couple of Our Favorite R & R Memories

Besides being stationed in various places, I took full advantage of R & R opportunities with Lisa and sometimes, the kids, and explored even more of the sites and foods of the world.

In the summer of 1986, for example, my family and I enjoyed the beautiful scenery and beaches of Jamaica for our R & R. My favorite memory from this trip was walking hand in hand as we explored the Otso Rios or 8 Rivers. We also found Jamaican cuisine incredible, and we couldn't believe the wide variety of native tropical fruits that were offered throughout town in markets or roadside carts.

The following summer, Lisa and I spent one week at Puerto Plata with two other couples: a Marine and a Navy corpsman and their spouses. We stayed in a stunning resort and went on many popular tourist adventures, including taking a cable car toward the Statue of Christ. When our tour guide let us visit the villages on our own, we tried their seafood offerings and explored quiet beaches that were recommended by the friendly and kind locals.

Notes for Context:

[1] MREs are shelf-stable rations used for consumption during military field operations. The standard MRE contains a main dish, crackers, salt and pepper, napkins, plastic utensils, and sometimes a warmer. Also, there is instant coffee with sugar and creamer, packets of peanut butter and jam, and cheese products for the entrées. Some favorites are spaghetti, eggs and ham, beef and gravy, etc. MREs have a shelf life of five years.

Chapter Fourteen

Our Legacy

As our children matured and came into their own, we've been amazed to witness how industrious and strong they have become. Lisa and I have been proudly watching them succeed career- and family-wise.

Analiz has been an educator in the Florida Broward County School District for over 26 years. She has taught high school health education, physical science, and environmental science. Analiz earned her BS in Health Education Science at Florida State University.

A year after the February 14, 2018 mass shooting at the Marjory Stoneman Douglas High School in Parkland, FL, she was selected to be trained by the Center of Mind-Body Wellness to help students who experience trauma. In addition to helping many youths, the GriefShare Ministries has helped her heal from her own personal trauma.

When she is not working and volunteering for GriefShare Ministries, she enjoys cycling outdoors and spending time at the beach. She has one son who is married and lives in Alabama.

She has received numerous commendations from her schools and former students. "As you get awards, God gives rewards."

My second daughter, Jennifer, graduated from Johns Hopkins University with a Master of Science in Information Systems and Telecommunications. She works for a commercial security software company and has over 15 years of security and privacy compliance experience.

Prior to making the jump over to the private sector, Jennifer was a public servant at the US Department of Health & Human Services' Cybersecurity Program, driving government-wide cloud computing adoption to help programs deliver their mission to the public in an innovative, secure, agile, and cost-efficient fashion. She is a recipient of the Fedl00 and Advanced Technology Academic Research Center (ATARC) Cloud Innovation awards.

Jennifer serves on the Carey Business School's Dean Alumni Association Board, which focuses on educational and philanthropy initiatives. She lives in Virginia with her husband and children.

Our youngest daughter, Evangeline, earned her bachelor's in political science at Florida State University. Soon after, she was commissioned as a 2nd Lieutenant in the United States Air Force and lived in Florida, Texas, and California.

After serving seven years, she resigned as Captain in the USAF and moved back to Florida. Evangeline spends her time as an insurance broker and volunteer at the community church. She is blessed with two loving sons. Her goal has always been to be independent and "master of none."

My one and only son, Joel, earned his bachelor's in finance at the University of North Florida and a master's in business administration at Jacksonville University. He currently works at Marion Public Schools District (MCPS). Prior to MCPS, he was the Director of Business Education and Corporate Training at St. Johns River State College for 10 years and worked in property and casualty insurance for 11 years.

Joel served on several non-profit boards that supported foster care, education, small business, and elder services. He is a gifted and talented communicator and has been invited as a guest speaker at numerous chamber events. I am blessed to witness his passion for promoting educational opportunities for all and encouraging businesses to seek local talent within the community.

Outside of his career, Joel enjoys fishing, home improvement projects, and spending time with family and friends. I am very happy that fishing turned out to be one of his hobbies because it was something special, and we both enjoyed it when he was a child.

Joel, Evangeline, Jennifer and Analiz

Chapter Fifteen

With Honor

I officially retired from the Navy on June 30, 1988. Captain T. W. Bone held my Battalion Formation Retirement Ceremony. Speeches were delivered by Division Officer CWO4 Geiger, the Chaplain, and Captain T. W. Bone himself. T.W. Bone spoke about my outstanding job as Division Petty Officer-In-Charge. He also commended me for my support of our Seabee Ball and the fundraising I helped with for three years.

Lisa was presented with a Letter of Appreciation from the United States Navy, which stated that she "has earned grateful appreciation for her unselfish and devoted service during her husband's Naval career. Her unfailing support and understanding helped to make possible her husband's lasting contribution to the nation." (Given the 19th Day of May 1988.) I can't express enough how much I appreciated Lisa. She was the anchor that kept the family stable and grounded while I was away. Also, she has been my biggest inspiration since we first met.

When my Seabee comrades took turns speaking during the ceremony, I started to get emotional. Their words were not only kind, they also made me realize that my military lifestyle, which is all I'd known my entire adult life to that point, was coming to a quick close.

I enjoyed every second I put into serving the country. All of the trainings, the tours of duty, building and maintaining infrastructure, and even the tiniest tasks truly were contributions toward the greater good. And all of it was my honor.

I am deeply humbled, as this was the path God had chosen for me. I learned and grew as a person, and I now have a loving family with whom I can continue my path.

MY HONORS AND AWARDS:

☆ Good Conduct (fifth)

☆ Meritorious Unit Commendation

☆ Battle E Ribbon

☆ National Defense Service Medal

☆ Vietnam Campaign Medal

☆ Republic of Vietnam Medal

☆ Overseas Service Ribbon 3 Awards

MEMBERSHIPS:

☆ Knights of Columbus 4th Degree 35 years

☆ Extraordinary Eucharistic Minister 18 years

☆ Lifetime Member of Disabled American Veterans

☆ Lifetime Member of Navy Seabee Veterans of America (CAN DO) "WE BUILD, WE FIGHT"

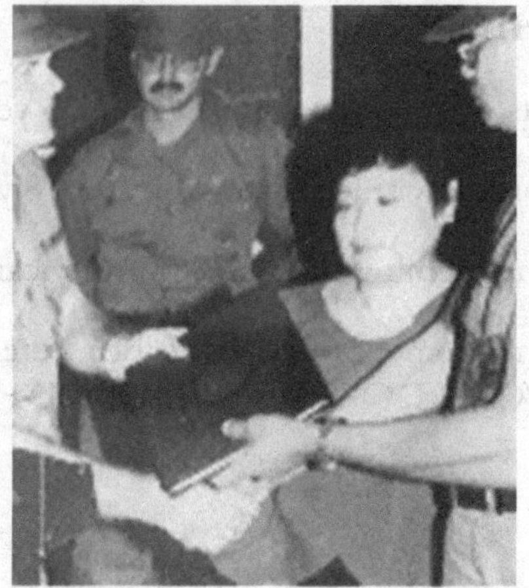

Lisa receives a well-deserved reward for her support and patience throughout my service.

CE1 Joey Abo is retiring from the United States Navy after 21 years of uninterrupted active duty.

A retirement ceremony was held for Abo today at McCalla Hangar. On June 30, 1988, Abo will transfer to the Fleet Re-

What an honor it was to serve our country.

Chapter Sixteen

Civilian Life

Jacksonville, Florida felt like a natural fit for retirement for our family. However, I still felt the need to be industrious, and while I didn't actively look, work somehow found me.

Just a few days after moving to Jacksonville, I was barely settled into my new surroundings and decided to check out the Navy Exchange (NEX). As I was making my way toward the entrance, I was approached by the Exchange's maintenance manager, Mr. Gate. He asked me if I had retired, and I responded that I retired as of June 30, 1988. Then he asked me if I would be interested in working for him.

Mr. Gate told me that he had heard of me - that I had worked part-time as an electrician in the Navy Exchange Maintenance Department, NAS, Jacksonville, when I was stationed with the Reserved Mobile Construction Battalion from September

1980 to September 1984. And they just happened to have a dire need for someone with this experience at that time.

Technically, we're supposed to wait at least six months after retirement before being re-employed, but he talked to people to see if there was any way to have me start sooner. Around August 1988, he was able to pull some strings and I started working for the Navy Exchange Maintenance Department.

While I was okay with this work, I yearned for more. I was friendly with our local postman, and after a few conversations, he encouraged me to apply for a position as a US Post Office employee. I passed an incredibly stringent written exam; however, I failed the physical exam after they found in my Navy medical records that I had elbow and back issues that would have affected my duties. I was disappointed and stayed with NEX Maintenance.

A couple of years later, in August of 1990, I left the Navy Exchange to start a position in the Clay County School Board maintenance department as an electrical technician. I was the only candidate with a Florida State license as an electrician holding a Master's certificate, so they made me an offer I could not refuse.

The school board provided many perks to employees and dependents, including part-time work for students during the summer. I thought that this would be a great opportunity for my kids to make money over the summer, enabling them to earn and save. Jennifer, Evangeline, and Joel took advantage of this opportunity and worked there throughout high school.

I Mean it This Time

In my lifetime, I have suffered from PTSD, back and neck pain, low vision in my right eye, tinnitus, and many other conditions, but nothing was more debilitating than my fight with prostate cancer.

My first pre-operational procedure was on March 26, 2004, and I started chemotherapy four days later. If you have or know anyone who has gone through radiation therapy, you probably know how excruciatingly painful this procedure is. It feels like your body is burning, you lose your appetite, and using the restroom can be painful.

Therapy was finally completed on July 8, 2004, but the pain and burning while urinating remained long after, as well as the constant urgency to use the bathroom. It was like torture, but I had to remind myself about Romans 5:3: Accept all suffering as part of our existence and experience as a human. This was a test of my faith.

Most importantly, I saw this as a sign that it was finally time for me to stop and rest. I put in for my retirement from the school board after working with them for 15 pleasant and productive years. They threw me a great and meaningful retirement party. Truly, 15 years was enough time to cultivate some wonderful, life-long friendships there.

I did not seek out employment or side jobs. As you can probably imagine, this was hard at first, but I was eventually able to relax and open my mind to the possibilities. My wife and I took this opportunity to cross off more places that were on our bucket list.

For R & R, we had previously traveled to Russia, China, Scotland, Greece, the West Indies, the Dominican Republic, and Jamaica. After retirement, we were able to cross off Jerusalem, Egypt, Portugal, France, and Italy from the list. The world is such a big place, and I am blessed to have been able to experience a good percentage of it.

Every so often, I reminisce about the random prophecy I received when I was playing outside with my friends and cousins as a junior high school student. It's been over half a century since then and indeed, *I went abroad.*

We *Build*.

We *Fight*.

Author's Notes:

The concept of a hero has become watered down through the generations. Many immediately visualize a "hero" as someone wearing a flashy outfit, possessing the abilities to fly, move mountains, and deflect bullets and lasers.

I'm not sure who coined the phrase, "Not all heroes wear capes." But if you run a search on the web or check out our country's history books, you'll find real-life heroes in drab green and camo, and clunky helmets. Many bear mental and physical scars along with disabilities from intense training or past battles, and they wear them proudly.

Joey may well be one of the few remaining Vietnam War veterans by the time of this publishing. While many questioned the Vietnam war at home, most involved understood why they were there: Loyalty to our country, freedom, respect, honor, and a sense of duty. They fought alongside comrades, trusting the mission was always for the greater good.

When I began to piece together Joey's story, a variety of emotions welled up inside of me. For example, anger a t f i r s t about Filipinos' treatment upon enlisting in the US Navy.

Joey, however, proved that there is never shame in hard work toward the mission. He was naturally industrious, and most importantly, he trusted God and His path for him. So, without question and doubt, he did his best and made good out of any situation.

Mr. Abo had mentioned one of his close friends when stationed in Honolulu, a fellow Seabee named Rene Angeles. Rene Angeles is my father. Out of a dozen Godparents, he and Lisa were the only ones who kept in touch with me throughout my childhood to the present.

Their second daughter, Jennifer, was my pen pal since I learned how to write. I remember distinctly the moment my dad encouraged me to send that first letter. We sent letters and pictures to each other a couple of times a month and met face-to-face shortly after graduating from college.

Jennifer and I reunited my parents with Ninong Joey and Ninang Lisa a couple of years before my father passed away. When they were together, they shared a meal and talked nonstop. Their hugs, pats on the back, and laughter were everything. I envisioned them as young couples in Honolulu navigating their way through life in a new world and as new parents together.

Growing up a military BRAT, I've learned that an honest man does not need to say he is honest to be viewed as honest. A brave man does not need to say he is brave to be considered brave. Nor does a hero need to call himself a hero to be perceived as a hero. It is in their actions and results of their actions that make them all of those things.

In the stories of his days as a soldier, as well as what I have witnessed in his everyday life, Joey Abo is all of the above. Rags to riches, a brother-in-arms, God-loving and God-fearing, a passionate husband, father, and grandfather. A model of dignity, strength, hard work, and grit. And to me, a faithful and loyal Godfather with many tales to tell.

Thank you for your service, Ninong Joey.

**Knights of Columbus
35 years, 4th Degree (2022)**

Sources

Below is a list of sources that were referenced for historical events mentioned throughout this memoir.

Our world would be a very different place without our nation's military and their dedication to our country's freedom.

1. Republic of the Philippines - Province of Abra:
https://abra.gov.ph/about/history/

2. "Projects by country or region - Philippines." Digital Museum, The Comfort Women's Issue and the Asian Women's Fund, Asian Women's Fund:
https://www.awf.or.jp/e3/philippine-01.html

3. Delgado, Anton L., Globe_, "National Animals: The Philippines: Carabao":
https://southeastasiaglobe.com/the-philippines-carabao/

4. Philippines Exchange Rate against USD:
https://www.ceicdata.com/en/indicator/philippines/exchange-rate-against-usd

5. Philippine News Agency Archives, "Today in Filipino history, November 3, 1934, Bannawag, a leading weekly Ilokano Magazine, was founded.":
http://kahimyang.com/kauswagan/articles/1327/today-in-philippine-history-november-3-1934-bannawag-a-leading-weekly-ilokano-magazine-was-founded

6. Naval History and Heritage Command, "Seabee History: Southeast Asia.": https://www.history.navy.mil/browse-by-topic/communities/seabees1.html

7. The LAWPHiL Project - Quezon, Manuel L (Former President), " BY THE PRESIDENT OF THE

PHILIPPINES [EXECUTIVE ORDER NO. 19, February 19, 1936]": https://www.history.navy.mil/browse-by-topic/communities/seabees1.html

8. Sicat, Gerardo P., Philippine Star, "Historical roots of urban squatting.": http://econ.upd.edu.ph/perse/?p=6719

9. Bureau of Naval Personnel, "Filipinos in the United States Navy, Prepared by: Bureau of Naval Personnel, October 1976.": https://www.history.navy.mil/research/library/online-reading-room/title-list-alphabetically/f/filipinos-in-the-united-states-navy.html

10. UNESCO Creative Cities Network. "Baguio City.": https://www.unesco.org/en/creative-cities/baguio-city

11. Portuguese Historical Museum, "The Hawaiian Connection.": http://portuguesemuseum.org/?page_id=2002&category=&exhibit=4&eve%20nt=

12. US Navy Seabee Museum, "Seabee Queens.": http://www.history.navy.mil/content/history/museums/seabee/explore/online-reading-room/seabee-faqs/seabee-queens.html#::text=Beginning%20in%201943%2C%20Seabees%20at,to%20preside%20over%20 the%20festivities

Disclaimer: These links were active at the time of this publishing. If the websites are no longer live, I encourage you to research these important historical events at the library or on the web.

*All photos were obtained from Joey Abo's personal collection.

As seen in Queen of Peace (formerly La Paz Catholic High School), La Paz, Abra, Philippines.

Joey Abo's Alma Mater dedicated their library, computer room, and lab to his legacy.